Power in My Pen

A Snippet of The Life of Ida B. Wells

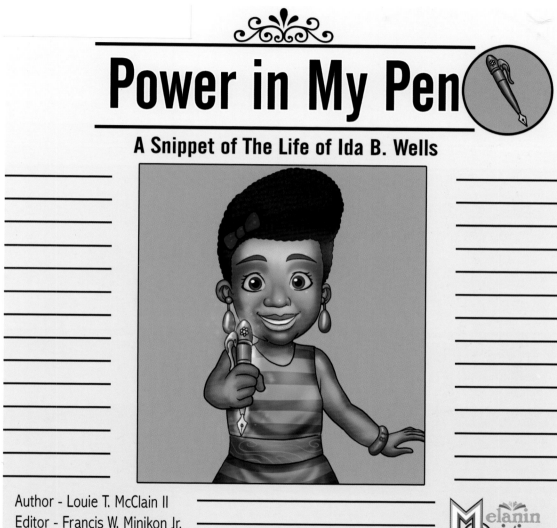

Author - Louie T. McClain II

Editor - Francis W. Minikon Jr.

Illustrator - M. Ridho Mentarie

Melanin Origins

Also from Melanin Origins:

"Flying Above Expectations" – Tuskegee Airmen Spring
"Free Your Mind" – Fredrick Douglass Fall 2017
"Louisiana Belle" – Madame C.J. Walker Spring 2017

Publisher's Cataloging-in-Publication
(Provided by Quality Books, Inc.)

McClain, Louie T., II, author.
Power in my pen : a snippet of the life of Ida B.
Wells / by Louie T. McClain II ; edited by Francis W.
Minikon Jr. ; illustrated by M. Ridho Mentarie.
pages cm
SUMMARY: A book about the life, accomplishments, and
achievements of Ida B. Wells, an inspirational
African-American journalist, leader, and innovator.
Audience: Ages 9 months to 5 years old.
ISBN 978-1-62676-905-2
1. Wells-Barnett, Ida B., 1862-1931--Juvenile
literature. 2. African American civil rights workers--
United States--Biography--Juvenile literature. 3. Civil
rights workers--United States--Biography--Juvenile
literature. 4. African Americans--Biography--Juvenile
literature. 5. African American women journalists--
United States--Biography--Juvenile literature.
6. African American women educators--Biography--Juvenile
literature. 7. United States--Race relations--Juvenile
literature. 8. Biographies. [1. Wells-Barnett, Ida B.,
1862-1931. 2. Civil rights workers. 3. Journalists.
4. African Americans--Biography. 5. Women--Biography.
6. Race relations.]   I. Mentarie, M. Ridho,
illustrator. II. Title.
E185.97.W55M33 2017   323.092
QBI16-900033

Dedication

I devote this piece of art to my amazing nieces Naomi Grace, Victory Rose, Taleah Faith, & Tahiri Hope. It is a surreal experience for me to be a patriarchal figure in our family and an ultimate blessing to watch you grow and mature into wonderful and outstanding young ladies. I want you to know that you are loved and that you are strong. Above all, I need for you to understand that God gave you a voice for a reason. Never succumb to silence and always use your talents to glorify Him. Stake your claim in this world.
— Louie T. McClain II

This book is dedicated to our nieces Aditi, Kyree, and Kaliah as well as our cousins Jasmah, Maya, Kayleigh, Ava, Heaven, Kelis, Reese, Imoney, and Yasmeen. These young girls are the future, and will do something tremendous to contribute to our world just as Ida B. Wells did. Their strength, leadership, and perseverance will be an inspiration to other young girls of this generation and the next one to come. We will watch as these young girls become women and inspire the world.
— Francis W. Minikon Jr.

This little pen of mine,
I'm going to let it shine!

INK

4

For there is power in my pen! When ink and paper meet together the world will know that my mind is clever.

5

My Granny told me that I am adored so much because I am a very strong girl.

After Mommy and Daddy became very ill, I made sure that my five brothers and sisters were cared for until they were all grown up.

Granny made the best tasting food in the whole wide world, and she always helped me cook for my brothers and sisters while I taught at the neighborhood school.

It was there in the classroom, filled with young bright minds, where I learned about the power that lies in my pen.

I greatly enjoyed teaching my students in the classroom.

Yet shortly after I began to teach, I was asked to write stories for the local newspaper!

12

Newspaper Stand

The readers loved the stories I wrote so much that the newspaper put me in charge of editing all the stories.

Editing simply means making sure everything comes out right - like when a teacher grades schoolwork.

My exceptional writing abilities paved the way for me to travel around the country and tell my stories to thousands of people.

I even traveled across the great Atlantic Ocean to Scotland and England to tell my stories as well.

I became the first African American woman in the entire Unites States to ever do that for a major newspaper.

Oh yes! There is mighty power in my pen, and I'll even let you in on a little secret my friend.

I believe that the secret to the power is always telling the truth, and never telling a fib.

You see, when I put my mighty pen to the paper, I always write about the things that matter the most to me - whether good or bad.

Granny always told me that I might not like everything that I hear or see, but no matter what I can do my best to make a difference.

At first I didn't understand what she meant, but I later realized that the candlelight of truth that Granny spoke of is the power that is found in my pen.

Everyone has a story to tell. Maybe one day the world will hear your stories too.

Just remember to always speak the truth. By doing so, you will show that true power flows from your brilliant mind down to your mighty powerful pen.

Power in My Pen Cursive Activity

Aa Bb Cc Dd Ee

Ff Gg Hh Ii Jj

Kk Ll Mm Nn

Oo Pp Qq Rr Ss

Tt Uu Vv Ww

Xx Yy Zz